EARTH DAY

by Linda Lowery • illustrations by Mary Bergherr
with a foreword by Gaylord Nelson

On My Own
HOLIDAYS
Revised Edition

Carolrhoda Books, Inc./Minneapolis

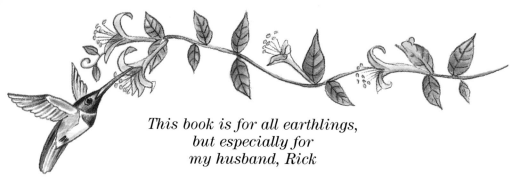

*This book is for all earthlings,
but especially for
my husband, Rick*

Special thanks to former Senator Gaylord Nelson
and the Wilderness Society as well as to Denis Hayes
and Green Seal, Inc.

Text copyright © 1991 by Linda Lowery, © 2004 by Linda Lowery
Illustrations copyright © 1991 by Carolrhoda Books, Inc., © 2004 by Carolrhoda Books, Inc.

This book is available in two editions:
Library binding by Carolrhoda Books, Inc., a division of Lerner Publishing Group
Soft cover by First Avenue Editions, an imprint of Lerner Publishing Group
241 First Avenue North
Minneapolis, Minnesota 55401 U.S.A.

Website address: www.lernerbooks.com

Library of Congress Cataloging-in-Publication Data

Lowery, Linda.
    Earth Day / by Linda Lowery ; foreword by Gaylord Nelson ; illustrations by
Mary Bergherr.— Rev. ed.
      p.   cm. — (On my own holidays)
    Summary: Explains, in simple text and illustrations, how and why Earth Day
became an international holiday calling global attention to the problems of pollution,
environmental destruction, and waste of natural resources.
    ISBN: 1–57505–700–X (lib. bdg. : alk. paper)
    ISBN: 1–57505–620–8 (pbk : alk. paper)
    1. Earth Day—Juvenile literature. 2. Environmentalism—Juvenile literature.
3. Environmental protection—Juvenile literature. [1. Earth Day. 2. Environmental
protection. 3. Holidays.] I. Bergherr, Mary, ill. II. Title. III. Series.
GE195.5.L69 2004
333.7'2—dc21   2002155961

Manufactured in the United States of America
1 2 3 4 5 6 – JR – 09 08 07 06 05 04

Foreword

Who wants to breathe dirty air or swim in a polluted lake? I don't, and I'm sure you don't either.

When I was a senator, I noticed that our country's air, water, and soil were getting polluted. Plants and animals were dying. People around the United States were upset about this. They wanted to change things. But our country's leaders were not listening. They were not making laws to protect the environment.

Finally, in June of 1969, I thought of an idea to get the attention of politicians. The idea was to have a nationwide demonstration. I thought that if enough people got involved, everyone from the president to each city's mayor would have to take notice.

And it worked. Twenty million Americans came out on Earth Day 1970 and showed they cared. The politicians finally started to listen.

But that was not good enough. The whole world needed to work together. So Earth Day 1990 was held. This time, people around the planet told their government officials that they wanted action to save our planet. Since then, Earth Day has been celebrated each year in countries all over the world. It has helped inspire people to make a difference and do their part.

Now it's your chance. In not too many years, you will be the people running the country. What you think and do matters. So learn about nature and respect it. Live in a way that cares for planet Earth. And keep after everyone from your mayor to the president to make laws that protect the planet. Your actions will make all the difference in the world.

Gaylord Nelson
founder of Earth Day
and former U.S. senator

In this huge universe,
there is one place
we can all call home.
It is the planet Earth.

Its lands are green and lively.
Its air is filled with oxygen
for us to breathe.
Everything we have
comes from Earth.

Our clothes, our food, and
the homes we live in come from Earth.
The medicines that make us well do, too.
Why not have a day
to celebrate our home,
the planet Earth?

Not long ago, a senator
from the state of Wisconsin
had that very idea.
His name was Gaylord Nelson.
During the 1960s,
Senator Nelson took many trips
across the country.
He saw Americans doing a lot of things
that harmed the planet.
They tossed litter
on the sidewalks and in the fields.
They drove their cars
as often as they could.
And their cars sent
poison gases into the air.

Farmers used chemicals on their crops
to make them grow.
The chemicals killed weeds and bugs.
The chemicals also killed
animals, fish, and birds.
Even bald eagles died.
Factories poured smoke into the skies,
turning them black.
Businesses and cities dumped trash
into lakes, rivers, and oceans.
All this spoiling of the land, air,
and water is called pollution.
Senator Nelson felt this damage
to our planet was wrong.
He wanted the United States to make
stronger laws to stop pollution.

Then, in 1969,
something big and awful happened.
An oil well sprang a leak
near Santa Barbara, California.
Millions of tons of oil
spilled into the Pacific Ocean.

The water turned dirty and smelly.
Pelicans, egrets, sea lions,
ducks, and other animals
became coated with thick, black oil.
Most of them died.

Senator Nelson was angry.

"Something must be done to stop this!"

he told students in California.

"We are destroying the very place

we live in and love."

What can we do to wake people up?

Senator Nelson wondered.

On the plane back to Washington, D.C.,

the senator had an idea.

What if Americans set aside one day

to learn how to care

for our troubled planet?

Maybe that day could be called Earth Day.

In the next days and weeks,

Senator Nelson called everyone he knew.

He told them about his idea.

Other Americans were angry

about pollution, too.

They wanted to help.

One of these people was

a law student named Denis Hayes.

Mr. Hayes said he would spend the year
helping the nation get ready
for Earth Day.
Other people offered to plan classes
and speeches in the places they lived.
Some wrote letters about pollution
to newspapers and magazines.
The word spread quickly.

On April 22, 1970,
the United States celebrated
the first Earth Day.
It was not a national holiday.
But it was the largest celebration
in Earth's history.

More than 20 million
Americans took part.
On that day, the United States Congress
did not meet.
Instead, the lawmakers went to classes
where they learned ways
to care for our planet.

Nearly every town and school
in the nation had special activities.
Scientists, doctors, store clerks,
police officers, factory workers, teachers,
students, and others took time off
to show their concern for planet Earth.
They marched.
They went to concerts.
They took nature walks
and studied about pollution.
Some people went to companies
that were polluting and asked them to stop.
In New York City,
the mayor stopped people
from driving cars on Fifth Avenue.
He wanted to show everyone how quiet
and clean the city could be.

The first Earth Day
was a great success.
People in the United States
began to litter less.
When they went to work,
they traveled together
in cars and buses.
Congress made stronger laws
and set up a new part of the government.
The new department was called the
Environmental Protection Agency (EPA).
Environment means the natural mix
of soil, water, air, climate, plants,
and animals in a certain place.
The EPA's job was to keep businesses,
cities, and states from polluting
our country's environment.

Soon the skies, the water, and the land
started to look cleaner.
More bald eagles were seen.

Ten years passed,
and Americans started to forget
the lessons of Earth Day.
They grew careless.
They began to waste
water, fuel, soil, and trees.
They acted as if these treasures
would never run out.

The United States government
was not keeping a careful
watch on pollution.

By now, pollution was harming more
than just the United States.
All over the planet,
poisons were quietly filling
the air, water, and land.

Businesses and governments
weren't getting rid of waste safely.
They thought it took too much time
and too much money.
They dumped more than ever.
They filled the air with smog
and the water with poisons.
Store owners changed swamps and
prairies into shopping malls.
Trees were burned to make farms.
Oil spills kept happening.
Rain forests, ice fields, deserts,
swamps, forests, and
prairies were being
spoiled or destroyed.

Garbage was piling up all around.

People bought things

and used them just once.

Then they threw them away:

diapers, soda cans,

plastic toys, and fast food packages.

Trucks carried the garbage

to enormous holes in the ground.

There the trash sat.

Some of it will be there forever.

Millions of acres of land

were being filled to the brim

with garbage.

And in the world's oceans,

thousands of tons of trash were floating

or had sunk to the bottom.

Creatures in every country were dying
because they had no place to live.
People were getting sick
from the poisons in the air and water.

Pollution was killing the planet,
and people were scared.
Something had to be done.

It was time for a world Earth Day.
Governments, businesses, and citizens
had to change how they were acting.
People from every nation needed
to be taught answers
for environmental problems.

For example, most garbage
can be made into new things.
This is called recycling.

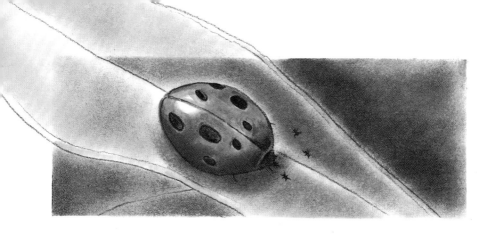

People don't need to use chemicals
on their crops and lawns.
There are safer, more natural ways
to protect plants and help them grow.
Ladybugs eat many insects that eat plants.
So do birds.
And plants grow strong and healthy
in dirt made from dead plants
and food scraps.
Rain forests don't have to be burned
or cut down to be useful.
They give us rubber, fruit, nuts,
medicines, and oxygen to breathe.

Since Earth Day 1970,
Denis Hayes had been teaching people
about things such as recycling
and farming without chemicals.
He had worked to make
tougher laws to protect
the water, air, soil, and animals.
Now he decided to work
on Earth Day 1990.
He called up many people
who had worked on the first Earth Day.
They all got busy again.
This time, their plans reached
far beyond the United States.

On April 22, 1990, 200 million people
in more than 140 countries
celebrated the second Earth Day.
Children around the world
formed cleanup teams.
They picked up litter
in the country and the cities.
In the United States,
T.V. programs showed what each person
could do to save our planet.
Americans marched, sang,
and spoke out for the environment.
In Nicaragua, young people
planted 10,000 fruit trees.
Schoolchildren in Sweden visited farms
that do not use chemicals on their crops.

Japan held a Garbage Festival.
People watched while garbage
was recycled into everything
from postcards to soap.
Thousands of people joined a Litter Walk
in New Brunswick, Canada.
In Jordan, the government decided
to plant a tree for every
new baby born in the country.

A team of mountain climbers
from the United States,
the Soviet Union, and China
met at Mount Everest.
As they climbed the mountain,
they picked up the trash
others had left behind.

Since 1990, more and more countries
have begun to take part in Earth Day.
From Kenya to Thailand, people have
found new ways to celebrate.
Some cities have day of peace,
with songs, prayers, and tree plantings.
Other cities have a car-free day.
People walk, bike, and
ride buses or trains to get places.
People who live near the ocean clean up
beaches and learn to care for the sea.

Each year on Earth Day,

hundreds of millions of people

work to repair the damaged Earth.

But one day is not enough

to fix many years of harm.

People around the world will have

to change their habits for good.

If they don't,

by the time you are grown up,

a lot of animals and plants,

clean air and fresh water

may be gone from Earth forever.

No one wants this to happen.

So world groups,

such as the United Nations,

are keeping up the work

of Earth Day.

Even countries that have disagreed

in the past are working together.

Scientists and government leaders

are sharing ideas.

Countries can do many things

to help the environment.

They can cut down on garbage

and plant more trees.

They can clean up the water and the air

and farm with few chemicals.

They can protect forests and animals

and use land more wisely.

People are working to make
worldwide laws to save our planet.
But world groups
cannot do the job alone.
Everyone must be part of the answer.
Every action we take
can help save Earth.
Or it can harm our planet some more.
So the next time you have a can of soda,
will you throw the can away?
Or will you recycle it?

43

Each April 22,

people celebrate Earth Day

in their towns, schools, and homes.

But why celebrate only once a year?

We can do better than that.

We can make every day an Earth Day.

If we do our share each day,

we WILL save the planet.

After all, Earth is

the only home we have.

It can't wait.

Can we?

At Home

Reuse things
Used things are cheaper and have that nice broken-in feel. Give your used toys and clothes to other children so they can enjoy them, too.

Make new soil
With help from an adult, mix fruit and vegetable scraps with leaves, grass, and twigs. Put them in a wire basket or special wooden box and let them sit outside. This is called composting. In the spring, the new soil can go in your garden or window box.

Recycle garbage
Save newspapers, cans, plastic and bottles. If your city doesn't pick up recyclables, call your city council or government offices and ask who does. Find out if plastic things are recycled in your area.

Save energy
Turn off the lights and the T.V. set when you leave a room.

Plant trees
Each tree cleans the air and makes new oxygen for us to breathe. It gives animals and insects places to make homes.

OFF